WRITING THAT CHANGED U.S. HISTORY

BILL OF RIGHTS

by Josephine Larsen

Pogo Books, an imprint of Jump! Library by FlutterBee

Ideas for Parents and Teachers

Pogo Books let children practice reading informational text while introducing them to nonfiction features such as headings, labels, sidebars, maps, and diagrams, as well as a table of contents, glossary, and index.

Carefully leveled text with a strong photo match offers early fluent readers the support they need to succeed.

Before Reading

- "Walk" through the book and point out the various nonfiction features. Ask the student what purpose each feature serves.
- Look at the glossary together. Read and discuss the words.

During Reading

- Have the child read the book independently.
- Invite them to list questions that arise from reading.

After Reading

- Discuss the child's questions. Talk about how they might find answers to those questions.
- Prompt the child to think more. Ask: Did you know about the Bill of Rights before reading this book? What more would you like to learn about your rights?

Pogo Books are published by Jump!
3500 American Blvd W, Suite 150
Bloomington, MN 55431
www.jumplibrary.com

Jump! is a division of FlutterBee Education Group.

Library of Congress Cataloging-in-Publication Data

Names: Larsen, Josephine author
Title: Bill of rights / by Josephine Larsen.
Description: Bloomington, MN: Jump!, Inc., 2026.
Series: Writing that changed U.S. history
Includes index.
Audience: Ages 7-10
Identifiers: LCCN 2025026874 (print)
LCCN 2025026875 (ebook)
ISBN 9798896623403 hardcover
ISBN 9798896623410 paperback
ISBN 9798896623427 ebook
Subjects: LCSH: Civil rights–United States–Juvenile literature | United States–United States. Constitution. 1st-10th Amendments–Juvenile literature
LCGFT: Law materials
Classification: LCC KF4750 .L37 2026 (print)
LCC KF4750 (ebook)
DDC 342.7308/5–dc23/eng/20250815
LC record available at https://lccn.loc.gov/2025026874
LC ebook record available at https://lccn.loc.gov/2025026875

Editor: Alyssa Sorenson
Designer: Emma Almgren-Bersie

Photo Credits: National Archives, cover (document); mato181/Shutterstock, cover (flag); SimoneN/Shutterstock, 1; ddukang/Adobe Stock, 3; Pictorial Press Ltd/Alamy, 4; Jack R Perry Photography/Shutterstock, 5; Bob Korn/Shutterstock, 6; Art Phaneuf/Alamy, 7; PRESSLAB/Shutterstock, 8-9; Sundry Photography/iStock, 10-11; MediaNews Group/Los Angeles Daily News/Getty, 12-13; moodboard/Getty, 14-15; Tom Williams/CQ-Roll Call, Inc/Getty, 16-17; Fred Schilling, Collection of the Supreme Court of the United States, 18; CarmenMurillo/iStock, 19; jacoblund/iStock, 20-21; John Arehart/Shutterstock, 23.

Printed in the United States of America at Corporate Graphics in North Mankato, Minnesota.

TABLE OF CONTENTS

CHAPTER 1

NEW RULES FOR A NEW COUNTRY

In 1776, the United States was a new country. **Congress** made the U.S. Constitution in 1787. It said how the **federal** government would run. But it did not say what **rights** people had.

Bill of Rights

Congress of the United States
begun and held at the City of New-York, on
Wednesday the fourth of March, one thousand seven hundred and eighty nine

States voted on what rights they wanted. They agreed on 10. These were added to the Constitution as **amendments**. They are the Bill of Rights. What are they? Let's find out!

CHAPTER 2

OUR RIGHTS

The First Amendment protects freedom of speech. This means people can say, write, and share what they want. They can **protest**. The government can't **punish** them for speaking out.

The First Amendment also says people can practice any **religion** they choose. The U.S. government can't tell people what religion to follow.

The Second Amendment says people have a right to own and use guns.

In the 1600s and 1700s, America belonged to Great Britain. British soldiers could legally take over homes. The Third Amendment says soldiers cannot do this anymore.

WHAT DO YOU THINK?

In the United States, adults have the right to own guns. They are used for hunting. They are sometimes used for protection or violence. Do you think people should be able to own guns? Why or why not?

HIGHWAY PATROL

Amendments Four through Eight protect people in trouble with the law. Police look for **evidence** after a crime. They search people's homes, cars, or other belongings. But they often need a **warrant** to do it. And they can't do it without a good reason. They also can't arrest someone without a good reason. Why? The Fourth Amendment says so.

judge
GARY POLK
JUDGE

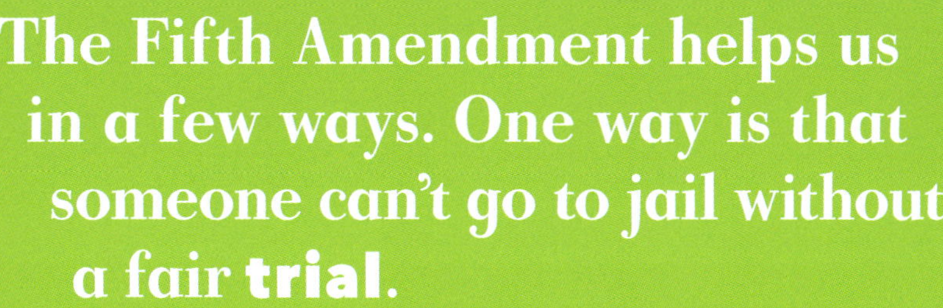

The Fifth Amendment helps us in a few ways. One way is that someone can't go to jail without a fair **trial**.

The Sixth Amendment says people get a trial. A trial shows the facts of a case. A judge or **jury** looks at the facts. They decide if the person is **guilty**.

DID YOU KNOW?

Part of the Fifth Amendment says people can't be charged for the same crime twice. If a judge or jury says a person is not guilty, the person can't go to trial again for that crime.

The Seventh Amendment gives people the right to a jury trial in some cases. Why is this important? A jury is made up of different people. They are not part of the government. Some people would rather have a jury decide if they are **innocent** or guilty.

The Eighth Amendment includes making sure the punishment for a crime isn't unfairly harsh.

jury

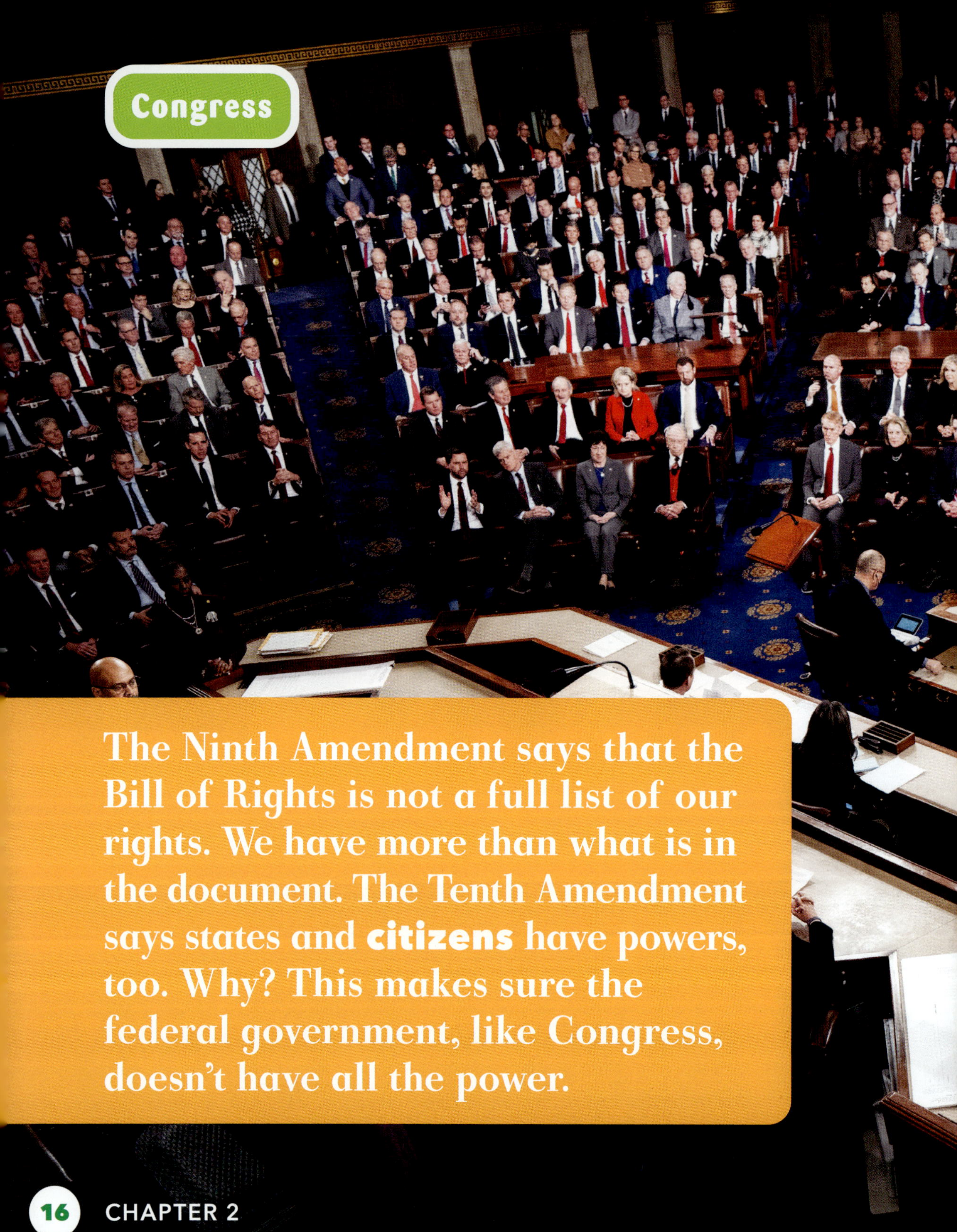

Congress

The Ninth Amendment says that the Bill of Rights is not a full list of our rights. We have more than what is in the document. The Tenth Amendment says states and **citizens** have powers, too. Why? This makes sure the federal government, like Congress, doesn't have all the power.

TAKE A LOOK!

How do the amendments protect us? Take a look!

INDIVIDUAL RIGHTS

1st Amendment
gives people freedom of speech and religion

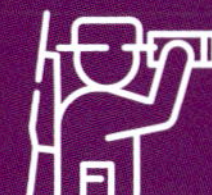

2nd Amendment
gives people the right to own and use guns

PROTECTION FROM POWER

3rd Amendment
stops soldiers from taking over citizens' homes

4th Amendment
stops police from searching and arresting without a good reason

9th Amendment
says people have more rights than what is in the Bill of Rights

10th Amendment
says states and citizens have powers

RIGHTS TO JUSTICE

5th Amendment
protects people charged with crimes

6th Amendment
gives people the right to a fast and fair trial

7th Amendment
gives people the right to a jury trial in some cases

8th Amendment
says people charged with crimes can't have harsh or unfair punishments

CHAPTER 3

THE SUPREME COURT

The government cannot ignore our rights. Supreme Court **justices** make sure of that. It is their job to make sure the Constitution is followed. How? Let's look at an example.

Supreme Court justices

In 2011, police took a man's cell phone **data**. Why? They wanted to see the phone's past locations. They saw that the phone was where many crimes happened. Police thought this meant the man did them. He got in trouble.

Let's END
CLIMATE
CHANGE

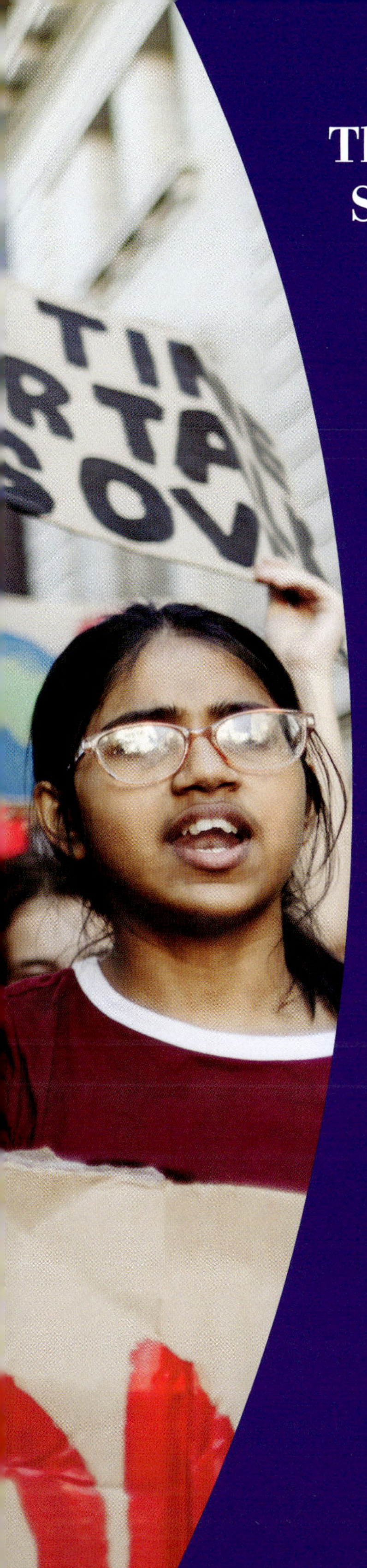

The man's case went to the Supreme Court. He said police did not have a warrant to get his phone's data. They didn't follow the Fourth Amendment. The Court agreed. Now, police often need a warrant to get phone data.

The Bill of Rights was written more than 200 years ago. It still protects our rights today. What right is most important to you?

WHAT DO YOU THINK?

Rights are meant to protect us and keep us safe. If you could make an amendment, what would it be? Why?

QUICK FACTS & TOOLS

TIMELINE

What are important dates in the history of the Bill of Rights? Take a look!

APRIL 19, 1775
America wants freedom from Great Britain. It needs to fight to do this. The Revolutionary War starts.

JULY 4, 1776
The United States forms.

SEPTEMBER 3, 1783
The United States wins the Revolutionary War. It is free from Great Britain.

1787
Congress makes the U.S. Constitution. It does not say what rights people have.

1789
James Madison is a member of Congress. He makes a list of rights. Congress agrees to send the rights to the states.

DECEMBER 15, 1791
The states agree to and approve the Bill of Rights.

GLOSSARY

amendments: Changes made to a law or legal document.

citizens: People who belong to a country and have full rights.

Congress: The part of the U.S. government that makes laws.

data: Information collected so something can be done with it.

evidence: Information and facts that help prove if something is true or false.

federal: Relating to the central government, under which states are united.

guilty: Responsible for a crime.

innocent: Not responsible for a crime.

jury: A group of people who listen to the facts during a trial and decide whether the charged person is innocent or guilty.

justices: Judges on the Supreme Court.

protest: To demonstrate against something.

punish: To issue a consequence for doing something wrong.

religion: A system of belief, faith, and worship.

rights: Things you are allowed to do.

trial: The examination of evidence in a court of law to decide if someone is guilty or innocent.

warrant: An official piece of paper that gives someone the right to do something.

INDEX

TO LEARN MORE

Finding more information is as easy as 1, 2, 3.

1. Go to www.factsurfer.com
2. Enter "Bill of Rights" into the search box.
3. Choose your book to see a list of websites.